W9-BIK-248

# SKITS & SCENES

Sharon Siamon
James Barry

Published in 1994 simultaneously by:

Nelson Canada,  *and*  The Wright Group
A Division of Thomson  19201 – 120th Avenue NE
  Canada Limited  Bothell, Washington
1120 Birchmount Road  98011-9512
Scarborough, Ontario  U.S.A.
M1K 5G4
Canada

ISBN 0-17-604364-0  ISBN 0-17-604397-7

1 2 3 4 5 /WC/ 97 96 95 94 93  1 2 3 4 5 /WC/ 97 96 95 94 93

I(T)P™
International Thomson Publishing
The trademark ITP is used under license

**Project Manager:** Lana Kong
**Senior Production Editor:** Deborah Lonergan
**Art Direction:** Bruce Bond
**Cover Design:** Stuart Knox
**Cover Illustration:** Russ Willms

Printed and bound in Canada

**Canadian Cataloguing in Publication Data**

Main entry under title:
Skits & scenes

(Nelson mini-anthologies)
ISBN 0-17-604364-0

1. Readers (Elementary). 2. Readers – American
drama. 3. American drama – 20th century.
4. Readers – Canadian drama (English).* 5. Canadian
drama (English) – 20th century.* I. Siamon, Sharon.
II. Barry, James, 1939–  . III. Series.

PE1127.D72S55  1994  812'.008  C93–095273–1

## Series Review Panel

# Table of Contents

## 1

## QUICK WARMUPS

## 2

## MONOLOGUES

# 3

## DIALOGUES AND SCENES

# 4

## SHORT PLAYS

# Quick Warm-ups

▲▼▶▼▶▲▼▶▼▶▲▼▶▼▶▲▼▶▼◀▶▶

Getting into the dramatic mode involves warming up the body, the voice, and the mind. Here are a few fun activities designed to get you started.

▲▼▶▼▶▲▼▶▼▶▲▼▶▼▶▲▼▶▼◀▶▶

▲ ▶ ▼ ▶ ▲ ▼ ▶ ▼ ▶ ▲ ▼ ▶ ▼ ▶ ▲ ▼ ▶ ▼ ▶ ▶

# MIRRORS

## by David W. Booth and Charles J. Lundy

In this exercise, your partner is your mirror, copying everything you do. Then, you become the mirror.

1. Choose a partner. One of you will be a "mirror." The other will stand in front of the mirror and move in slow motion, using only hands and arms at first. As the "mirror" becomes more confident in copying your movements, expand your movements to include your whole body. Change roles often so that each of you gets lots of practice being both the mirror and the reflected person.

2. The person in front of the mirror is getting dressed to go to a costume party. Decide what your costume is but do not tell your partner. After you have put the costume on, the mirror image has to describe the costume and guess what it is.

▲▼▶▼▶▲▼▶▼▶▲▼▶▼▶▲▼▶▼▶

# IT COULD BE WORSE

## by Larry Swartz

It's fun to think of "it could be worse" situations. How about class trips, school dances, or that old favourite, the family vacation!

Each partner should tell an "it could be worse" story.

## Example

MEL: What a trip I had. First, I thought I lost my tickets for the plane.

BELLE: It could be worse.

MEL: The taxi got lost on the way to the airport.

BELLE: It could be worse.

MEL: I left my luggage in the taxi.

BELLE: It could be worse.

**MEL:** The plane was three hours late.

**BELLE:** It could be worse.

**MEL:** The stewardess announced that there was a bomb on the plane.

**BELLE:** It could be worse.

▲▼▶▼▲▼▶▼▲▼▶▼▲▼▶▼▼▶▶

# FORTUNATELY/ UNFORTUNATELY

## by Peter Moore

This is another quick-response word game. Don't throw in anything that breaks the flow of ideas on the topic—what you add has to be possible, if highly unlikely.

Circles of five to seven (preferable to have odd numbers).

One person starts with a statement.

The next person around the circle adds a sentence beginning with *Fortunately*.

The next person adds a sentence beginning with *Unfortunately* ... and so on.

For example:

On Saturday I went to the beach.
*Fortunately* I took my suntan lotion.
*Unfortunately* I forgot my bathing suit.
*Fortunately* ... and so on.

Once again you must listen carefully to what has already been said or what you add will not follow logically.

# TONGUE TWISTERS

## Collected by Anna Scher and Charles Verrall

Tongue twisters provide an ideal verbal warm-up. Four repetitions are enough for the one-liners. Writing your own tongue twister might be an interesting challenge.

1. Six sleek swans swam swiftly southwards.

2. Mixed biscuits

3. Richard gave Robin a rap in the ribs for roasting his rabbit so rare.

4. Harry from Hampstead hangs his hat on a hanger,

   Hannah hangs hers on a hook in the hall.

5. Three grey geese in a green field grazing,

   Grey were the geese and green was the grazing.

6. How much wood would a woodchuck chuck
   If a woodchuck could chuck wood?

7. Five flies flew round the farmyard
   Frightening the farmer's friend.

8. If a good cook could cook cuckoos
   How many cuckoos could a good cook cook
   If a good cook could cook cuckoos?

9. Three fiddling pigs sit in a pit and fiddle,
   Fiddle piggy, fiddle piggy, fiddle piggy.

10. I can think of thin things,
    Six thin things, can you?
    Yes I can think of six thin things
    And of six thick things too.

11. Double bubble gum bubbles double.

12. Bed spreaders spread beds.
    But bread spreaders spread bread.

13. Which is the witch that wished the wicked wish?

14. If you notice this notice you'll notice this notice is not worth noticing.

# 2

# Monologues

▲▼▶▼▶▲▼▶▼▶▲▼▶▼▶▲▼▶▼▶▲▼▶▶

*"To be, or not to be:*
*That is the question."*
Hamlet

These lines start the most famous monologue in drama. A *monologue* is a speech
for a single actor (the prefix *mono-* means
"one"). In a monologue, a character
expresses what he or she is thinking or
feeling.

Sometimes the character is alone on
stage, talking aloud to himself or herself as
if the audience were not there. Sometimes
the character speaks to other characters on
stage, or perhaps addresses an unseen
person. And sometimes the character talks
directly to *you*, in the audience.

▲▼▶▼▶▲▼▶▼▶▲▼▶▼▶▲▼▶▼▶▲▼▶▶

▲ ▶ ▼ ▲ ▶ ▼ ▲ ▶ ▼ ▲ ▶ ▼ ▲ ▶ ▼ ▲ ▶ ▼ ▲ ▶ ▶

# I HAD TO GO

## by Elizabeth Swados

A. J. is a character from *Runaways*, a musical play about teenagers living in the streets. The play looks at the anger and loneliness of the young characters, and their ways of coping with the world. Many of the monologues and short scenes in the play were improvised by the actors in the first production.

*A. J. dashes onto the stage as if being chased by a siren. . . . Three actors with parent masks stand above him on a platform. A. J. speaks to the audience.*

**A. J.:** My parents lived together, but they hated each other. See, my father went to work, see, he was the head of the family. And Mom, it was her job to stay home all day and clean the house. And every night at about six o'clock, I'd hear the electric garage door open, and I'd think to myself:

"Did I do everything right? Did I do everything right?" Then I'd hear him come up the stairs. This was it! Please don't yell, Dad. Please don't yell. Then Mom would call us, and we'd all go sit at the table. And there'd be silence, until my father would say something stupid. And my mother would break down and they'd start fighting, and she'd grab us and put our coats on and try to take us out the door, and my father would pull us back in and leave my mother out on the porch all by herself. And I was tired of being fought over. I had to go! I had to go!

# LITTLE LEAGUE DREAMER

by Peg Kehret

**Team sports are supposed to be fun—but not if the coach believes that winning is more important than how you play the game.**

Someday, I'm going to coach a Little League baseball team. When I do, I'm going to let everybody have a turn to play in every game. No. Not just a turn to play; everybody's going to have a turn to *start*.

I go to all the practices, but I hardly ever get to play in the games. I just sit on the bench and watch and yell for the other guys. Oh, once in a while I get to go in, but it's usually the last inning and we're either so far ahead that there's no way we can blow it, or else we're so far behind that there's no way we can catch up. If the game is close at all, I never get a turn to play.

On the first day of practice, the coach asked

all of us what position we wanted to play. Most of the guys wanted to be the pitcher, but I said I wanted first base, so he put me at first base. I was doing great until two ground balls got by me. Then I caught a pop fly, but when I threw to third, to get the runner there, I overthrew and the runner scored. After that, I didn't get to play first base anymore, which really isn't fair because those were just mistakes and I would never make them again.

Although I prefer to play first base, I'd be happy with centre field or any other position. I'm not fussy.

The coach says he puts Ricky Anders at first base because Ricky's arm is better than mine and so is his batting average. That may be true, but the reason Ricky's arm is better and he gets more hits is because he plays more. I'd be a better hitter if I got a chance more often. I admit I don't hit so well in practice, but that's different. I know I'd be great if I had a chance to hit during a game.

Once, I actually got up to bat during the last inning of a game. The batter ahead of me walked, so there was a runner on base. I knew it was my big chance. I couldn't win the game—we were already eleven runs ahead—but if I could hit a home run, it would show the coach how good I really am. Maybe he'd even let me start next time.

I didn't get the home run. I didn't even get a

single. What I got was a strike-out, on a called strike three when I wasn't even swinging. I'll never make that mistake again, either, but the coach just won't listen.

It's such a waste of talent. I know I could be an All-Star baseball player, if only I got to play more often.

▲ ▼ ◄ ▲ ▼ ► ◄ ▲ ▼ ► ◄ ▲ ▼ ► ◄ ▲ ▼ ► ◄ ▶

# WAITRESS!

## by Vernon Howard

In this monologue, the actor plays two roles:
the waitress (or waiter) and the customer.
Although this skit could easily be used as a
dialogue, it is much funnier with a single
actor constantly sitting down as the diner and
jumping up to deliver the server's lines.

## CHARACTERS

WAITRESS, or WAITER, and DINER (double role). As
DINER, sit in a chair, preferably at a table. As
WAITRESS, stand up.

**WAITRESS:** (*to* DINER *at table*) Good evening, Ma'am,
what would you like for dinner?

**DINER:** How about a menu?

**WAITRESS:** (*writing*) One menu ... will you have it

with potatoes or peas?

DINER: Potatoes, please...

WAITRESS: (*surprised*) Potatoes *and* peas? ... You can't have *both*.

DINER: I said potatoes, *please*. I'm just trying to be polite. All I said was *please*.

WAITRESS: (*shrugging*) One menu with peas ... and what do you want in your coffee?

DINER: Sugar, please.

WAITRESS: (*writing*) A cup of coffee with sugar peas... (*shrugging*) Everyone to his own taste... (*sets bowl on table*) Here's your soup—please don't slurp.

DINER: (*frowning*) Waitress, this soup is too hot.

WAITRESS: (*stirring soup with finger*) How's *that*?

DINER: (*frowning*) Now it's too *cold*.

WAITRESS: (*shrugs, pretends to strike match on shoe, drops lit match in bowl*) There you are!

DINER: Where's the soup spoon?

WAITRESS: (*holds bowl to* DINER'S *lips, tilts*) Big shortage of spoons today!

DINER: (*angry*) You spilled the soup on my clothes! Get some water!

WAITRESS: (*pretends to pour water glass over* DINER'S *head*) There you are, all nice and clean!

DINER: Tell me, do you have any spareribs?

WAITRESS: (*carefully counts her ribs with forefinger*) No, just the usual number.

DINER: I'm simply starving for some *good food*. What do you suggest?

WAITRESS: Try the restaurant next door.

DINER: Come, come … how are your stuffed peppers?

WAITRESS: (*amazed, leans near* DINER) Would you please repeat that?

DINER: I said, how are your stuffed peppers?

WAITRESS: (*shakes some pepper into hand, stares at it*) You mean these little things can actually be *stuffed?*

DINER: (*impatient*) Young lady, will you please call the head waiter?

WAITRESS: What shall I call him?

DINER: Don't you have some salad with fancy seasonings?

WAITRESS: *Fancy* seasonings?

DINER: That's what I said—*fancy* seasonings.

**WAITRESS:** (*takes various seasonings, whirls fancily about, shakes onto plate*) Fancy salt… (*shakes from high up*) Fancy pepper… (*shakes backward over head*) Fancy nutmeg… (*shakes while swaying on one foot*) Fancy cinnamon… (*shakes from behind* DINER) Fancy garlic salt… (*shakes with dipping motions*) Fancy poppy seeds… (*shakes with crossed arms*) Is that *fancy* enough?

**DINER:** Never mind. Bring me some pie … maybe you'd better bring *two* pieces.

**WAITRESS:** (*eager*) *Two* pieces?

**DINER:** Yes, *two* pieces. I'm hungry.

**WAITRESS:** (*puts two pieces at plate, sits alongside* DINER, *points to pie*) Which piece do *you* want?

**DINER:** Go away, let me eat in peace… (*eats hungrily*)

**WAITRESS:** (*hovering over*) Yum-yum, that sure looks *good.*

**DINER:** (*ignoring her*) Delicious!

**WAITRESS:** (*smacking lips*) Oh, boy, wish *I* could have a bite.

**DINER:** (*annoyed*) Do you really want some?

**WAITRESS:** Yum-yum *yummy!*

**DINER:** (*picks up imaginary pie and plate, pushes pie in*

Waitress's *face)* How's *that?*

**Waitress:** *(smacks lips, draws fingers over smeared face)*
Yum-yum yummy and *yum-yum-yum!*

**Diner:** What kind of pie *is* this?

**Waitress:** *(licking fingers) Squash* pie!

*Bow and exit.*

▲ ▼ ▼ ▶ ▲ ▼ ▶ ▼ ▶ ▲ ▼ ▶ ▼ ▶ ▲ ▼ ▶ ▼ ▶ ▶

# THE LIFE AND TIMES OF HUMPTY DUMPTY

## by Martha Bolton

A spoof pokes fun at a well-known subject. What if a news reporter were at the scene to record the tragic day Humpty Dumpty fell off the wall?

## CHARACTER

NEWS REPORTER (male or female)

## SETTING

A mock brick wall

## PROPS

A hand-held microphone

## COSTUME

Business attire

NEWS REPORTER *is standing in front of the brick wall, holding the microphone and looking into an imaginary television camera.*

Ladies and gentlemen, I am here standing in front of the very wall off which Mr. Dumpty, "Humpty" to his many friends and fans, fell earlier today. This is a most tragic and solemn moment.

Our mini-cams were on the scene within minutes of the accident, and have remained here throughout the day while all the king's horses and all the king's men attempted to put Humpty Dumpty back together again. Let's see if we can talk to one of them now.

(REPORTER *mimes working his/her way through crowd.*) Excuse me, sir, but just how serious does it look for Mr. Dumpty? ... You say it could go either way? He could fully recover or be Eggs Benedict by morning? Only time will tell? (*sighs*) Well, sir, I want to commend you and the other king's men on all that you've done. I've been watching you guys scrambling around here—no pun intended—making sure everything that can be done is being done. And I even understand some of the nation's top Crazy Glue specialists have been called in and are working around the clock. One thing's for certain, Humpty Dumpty is in the best of hands!

(*Into camera*) And so, while we await word of Humpty Dumpty's condition, our station felt this would be a good time for a retrospective of his illustrious and legendary career.

After being discovered in the dairy case of a

Hollywood grocery store, Humpty was cast in a supporting role in the film classic "Cheaper By The Dozen." From there he moved on to star in such notable movies as "The Breakfast Club," "The Egg Who Came To Dinner," and what many have termed his finest film, "The Good, The Bad, and The Hard-Boiled."

Humpty was a private person. No matter how hard you tried, you just couldn't seem to get past his outer shell. He was a well-rounded individual, and even though some say he wasn't all he was cracked up to be, he was still considered a "good egg" by those who knew him best.

He never complained when we'd paint him funny colours at Eastertime or toss his relatives around at a picnic.

Yes, Humpty Dumpty (*wiping a tear from his/her eye*), you're quite a guy! And wherever you are right now, I hope you know we're all rooting for you! … I'd throw in, "and that's no 'yoke,' " but I'm sure in your line of work, you've been around enough hams.

So, let me just close by saying, "Good luck, and always remember to keep your sunny side up!"

This is (*fill in your name*) reporting from (*fill in city*). Good night.

*Blackout.*

# 3

# Dialogues and Scenes

*"Here's looking at you, kid."*
*Humphrey Bogart in* Casablanca

Even if you haven't seen the movie, you've probably heard the line. Dialogue—the lines spoken by actors—is perhaps the most essential part of a play, a movie, a TV or radio script. Every dramatist tries to create memorable lines for characters.

A *dialogue* is a conversation between two or more actors (the prefix *dia-* means "two"). Dialogues reveal the interaction between the characters, which is what drama is all about. Are the characters in love? friends? enemies? Are they being polite to each other or having a fight? Listening carefully to dialogues will tell you about the characters' personalities and their relationship with one another.

▲▶▾▲▶▾▲▶▾▲▶▾▲▶▾▲▶▾▲▶▾▲▶▾

# ENVY

## by Joan Sturkie and Marsh Cassady

It's easy to dismiss someone when you think they have everything. But what if you got to know them better?

## CHARACTERS

FAITH  
LORI  } three teenagers  
BRAD

*The action takes place in the school cafeteria at lunchtime. FAITH and LORI are sitting across from each other at a long table. At the far end is BRAD. Finishing his lunch, BRAD picks up his tray and walks past the girls.*

**BRAD:** Hi, Faith. Lori. How you doing?

FAITH: Hi, Brad. That was a quick lunch.

BRAD: Growing boys like me work up an appetite.
*FAITH laughs, but LORI is not amused.*

LORI: (*mocking*) "Growing boys like me." (*in a normal tone*) Who does he think he is, anyhow?

FAITH: Brad?

LORI: Yeah, Brad. He's nothing but a spoiled brat.

FAITH: (*surprised*) I gather you don't like him.

LORI: The boy who has everything? I'm afraid not.

FAITH: So he's rich, so what?

LORI: Why are you defending him all of a sudden?

FAITH: What's wrong with him? I like him. Maybe you just don't know him.

LORI: What's to know?

FAITH: Like I said, he's a good kid.

LORI: He can afford to be. He can afford anything he wants.

FAITH: I get it. Just because he has a rich dad, that makes him a jerk.

LORI: That isn't what I said.

FAITH: I think you're jealous.

LORI: So what if I am?

FAITH: Look, Lori, Brad can't help who his parents are.

LORI: What is this? Is he your boyfriend?

FAITH: You know better than that.

LORI: You mean, why would a boy from the rich part of town go for a girl like you?

FAITH: No, that isn't what I mean. I mean that he's just a friend.

LORI: You call him a friend. He's nothing but an egotistical—

FAITH: He is not.

LORI: (*surprised*) Why are you sticking up for him so much?

FAITH: Why are you attacking him?

LORI: I don't have to listen to this. I thought we were friends. I thought we cared about each other. And you choose that ... that stuck-up goon over me.

LORI *jumps up, grabs her tray, and stalks off. For a moment* FAITH *sits by herself, randomly jabbing a fork into what's left of her lunch. She doesn't see* BRAD *coming back.*

**Brad:** Mind if I sit down?

**Faith:** I thought you'd gone.

**Brad:** Just cleaning off my tray. (*sitting beside her*) I couldn't help but hear what was going on. I mean, I wasn't trying to eavesdrop, but Lori's voice *does* carry. (*pause*) It's kind of dumb, but anyhow, thanks.

**Faith:** Lori can't help it, I guess. It's just the way she is. But you can't help it either.

**Brad:** I suppose everyone is envious of someone. Or something.

**Faith:** Maybe. But most of the time, it's just a passing thought. Except maybe for young kids.

**Brad:** (*smiling*) You know who I envy?

**Faith:** Who?

**Brad:** You, and, well, Lori too.

**Faith:** For heaven's sake, why?

**Brad:** I've never talked about this to anyone before. But sometimes I wish I could escape. Sure, I like to be able to get pretty much what I want, but...

**Faith:** But what?

**Brad:** This is really weird. I have this darned ... responsibility, I guess. This thing where, somehow, I have to be perfect, you know?

FAITH: What do you mean?

BRAD: There are lots of people like Lori. I mean, in the respect that they're envious.

FAITH: Jealous, you mean.

BRAD: Okay, then, jealous. Anyhow, I feel as if they're judging me all the time. There's this gigantic spotlight following me everywhere I go. (*laughs*) Not really, but because of my background, my family, everything I do is judged. Is looked at. I hate it. Once in a while, I just want to be me. I just want to be like everyone else.

FAITH: Wow. I never would have thought of that.

BRAD: Sure, having parents who are well off is pretty darned nice, most of the time. I'm the first to admit it. But at other times ... I'd just like to be one of the crowd. You know?

▲▼▶▼▲▼▶▼▲▼▶▼▲▼▶▼▲▼▶▶

# WHO'S ON FIRST?

## by Bud Abbott and Lou Costello

This classic comedy skit was presented to the Baseball Hall of Fame in Cooperstown, N. Y. in 1956.

*Note:* The skit has been divided into five parts to allow multiple readers.

1

ABBOTT: You know, strange as it may seem, they give ball players nowadays very peculiar names. Now, on the Cooperstown team we have Who's on first, What's on second, I Don't Know is on third...

COSTELLO: That's what I want to find out. I want you to tell me the names of the fellows on the Cooperstown team.

ABBOTT: I'm telling you. Who's on first, What's on second, I Don't Know is on third…

COSTELLO: You know the fellows' names?

ABBOTT: Yes.

COSTELLO: Well then, who's playing first?

ABBOTT: Yes.

COSTELLO: I mean the fellow's name on first base.

ABBOTT: Who.

COSTELLO: The fellow's name on first base for Cooperstown.

ABBOTT: Who.

COSTELLO: The guy on first base.

ABBOTT: Who is on first base.

COSTELLO: Who is on first base?

ABBOTT: Who is on the first base.

COSTELLO: Well, what are you asking me for?

2

ABBOTT: I'm not asking you, I'm telling you. Who is on first.

COSTELLO: I'm asking you—Who's on first?

**ABBOTT:** That's the man's name.

**COSTELLO:** That's whose name?

**ABBOTT:** Yes.

**COSTELLO:** Well, go ahead, tell me!

**ABBOTT:** Who.

**COSTELLO:** The guy on first.

**ABBOTT:** Who.

**COSTELLO:** The first baseman.

**ABBOTT:** Who is on first.

**COSTELLO:** Have you got a first baseman on first?

**ABBOTT:** Certainly.

**COSTELLO:** Well, all I'm trying to do is find out what's the guy's name on first base.

**ABBOTT:** Oh, no, no. What is on second base.

**COSTELLO:** I'm asking you who's on second.

**ABBOTT:** Who's on first.

**COSTELLO:** That's what I'm trying to find out.

**ABBOTT:** Well, don't change the players around.

**COSTELLO:** I'm not changing anybody.

**ABBOTT:** Now take it easy.

COSTELLO: What's the guy's name on first base?

ABBOTT: What's the guy's name on second base.

COSTELLO: I'm not asking ya who's on second.

ABBOTT: Who's on first.

COSTELLO: I don't know.

ABBOTT: He's on third. We're not talking about him.

COSTELLO: How could I get on third base?

ABBOTT: You mentioned his name.

COSTELLO: If I mentioned the third baseman's name, who did I say is playing third?

ABBOTT: No, Who's playing first.

COSTELLO: Stay offa first, will you?

ABBOTT: Please. Now what is it you want to know?

3

COSTELLO: What is the fellow's name on third base?

ABBOTT: What is the fellow's name on second base.

COSTELLO: I'm not askin' ya who's on second.

ABBOTT: Who's on first.

COSTELLO: I don't know. (*makes noises*) You got an outfield?

ABBOTT: Oh, sure.

COSTELLO: Cooperstown has got a good outfield?

ABBOTT: Oh, absolutely.

COSTELLO: The left fielder's name?

ABBOTT: Why.

COSTELLO: I don't know. I just thought I'd ask.

ABBOTT: Well, I just thought I'd tell you.

COSTELLO: Then tell me who's playing left field.

ABBOTT: Who's playing first.

COSTELLO: Stay out of the infield.

ABBOTT: Don't mention any names out here.

COSTELLO: I want to know what's the fellow's name in left field.

ABBOTT: What is on second.

COSTELLO: I'm not asking you who's on second.

ABBOTT: Who is on first.

COSTELLO: I don't know. (*makes noises*)

ABBOTT: Now take it easy, man.

COSTELLO: And the left fielder's name?

ABBOTT: Why.

COSTELLO: Because.

ABBOTT: Oh, he's centre field.

COSTELLO: Wait a minute. You got a pitcher on the team?

ABBOTT: Wouldn't this be a fine team without a pitcher?

COSTELLO: I don't know. Tell me the pitcher's name.

ABBOTT: Tomorrow.

COSTELLO: You don't want to tell me today?

ABBOTT: I'm telling you, man.

COSTELLO: Then go ahead.

ABBOTT: Tomorrow.

COSTELLO: What time?

4

ABBOTT: What time what?

COSTELLO: What time tomorrow are you gonna tell me who's pitching?

ABBOTT: Now listen. For the last time, Who is not pitching, Who is on—

COSTELLO: I'll break your arm if you say who's on first.

ABBOTT: Then why come up here and ask?

COSTELLO: I want to know what's the pitcher's name.

ABBOTT: What's on second.

COSTELLO: I don't know. Ya got a catcher?

ABBOTT: Yes.

COSTELLO: The catcher's name?

ABBOTT: Today.

COSTELLO: Today, and Tomorrow is pitching.

ABBOTT: Now you've got it.

COSTELLO: That's all? Cooperstown's got a couple of days on their team. That's all?

ABBOTT: Well, I can't help that.

COSTELLO *makes noises*.

ABBOTT: All right. What do you want me to do?

COSTELLO: Gotta catcher?

ABBOTT: Yes.

COSTELLO: I'm a good catcher too, you know.

ABBOTT: I know that.

COSTELLO: I would like to play for the Cooperstown team.

ABBOTT: Well, I might arrange that.

COSTELLO: I would like to catch. Now I'm being a

good catcher. Tomorrow's pitching on the team and I'm catching.

ABBOTT: Yes.

COSTELLO: Tomorrow throws the ball, and the guy up bunts the ball.

ABBOTT: Yes.

COSTELLO: Now, when he bunts the ball—me being a good catcher—I want to throw the guy out at first base, so I pick up the ball and throw it to who?

ABBOTT: Now, that's the first thing you've said right.

COSTELLO: I DON'T EVEN KNOW WHAT I'M TALKING ABOUT!

ABBOTT: Well, that's all you have to do.

## 5

COSTELLO: I throw it to first base?

ABBOTT: Yes.

COSTELLO: Now, who's got it?

ABBOTT: Naturally.

COSTELLO: Who has it?

ABBOTT: Naturally.

COSTELLO: Naturally.

ABBOTT: Naturally.

COSTELLO: I throw the ball to Naturally?

ABBOTT: You throw the ball to Who.

COSTELLO: Naturally.

ABBOTT: Naturally. Well, say it that way.

COSTELLO: That's what I'm saying!

ABBOTT: Now don't get excited. Now don't get excited.

COSTELLO: I throw the ball to first base.

ABBOTT: Then Who gets it.

COSTELLO: He better get it.

ABBOTT: That's it. All right now, don't get excited. Take it easy.

COSTELLO: Hmmmmmph.

ABBOTT: Hmmmmmph.

COSTELLO: Now I throw the ball to first base, who grabs it, so the guy runs to second.

ABBOTT: Uh-huh.

COSTELLO: Who picks up the ball and throws it to what. What throws it to I don't know. I don't know throws it back to tomorrow—a triple play.

**ABBOTT:** Yeah. It could be.

**COSTELLO:** Another batter gets up and it's a long fly ball to centre. Why? I don't know. And I don't care.

**ABBOTT:** What was that?

**COSTELLO:** I said, I don't care.

**ABBOTT:** Oh, that's our shortstop.

COSTELLO *makes noises, throws bat angrily, steps closer to* ABBOTT, *and they glare at each other.*

### The Cooperstown Team

First baseman: Who
Second baseman: What
Third baseman: I Don't Know
Left fielder: Why
Centre fielder: Because
Pitcher: Tomorrow
Catcher: Today
Shortstop: I Don't Care
Right fielder: (no name given)

▲▼▶▼▶▲▼▶▼▶▲▼▶▼▶▲▼▶▼▶▶

# JOCK TALK:
# A RADIO INTERVIEW

### by Jeff Siamon

Everyone has heard the annoying sports
interviewer who won't let the athlete get a
word in edgewise. In this skit, the interviewer
finally gets the reward he so richly deserves.

## CHARACTERS

JOHNNY C., a fast-talking radio sports announcer
BUDDY HOWLER, captain of the Wallabee
    Woodchucks hockey team

## SETTING

The dressing room of the Wallabee Woodchucks

*Note:* This is a radio play or skit. It is meant to be
read, not acted out in front of an audience. While it
is not necessary to have sound effects, they can be
added to make the skit sound more real.

*We hear the sounds of a crowded dressing room.*

JOHNNY: Hello everybody, this is your favourite announcer, Johnny C., talking to you live from the Wallabee Woodchucks' dressing room. It's like a dream come true. Tonight, after thirty-nine years of trying, the Woodchucks have won their first league title, beating the Tomaine Tornadoes by a score of five to four. Standing next to me is the Woodchucks' leading goal-scorer and team captain, Buddy Howler. Well, I guess, Buddy, you guys are pretty happy now that the Woodchucks have finally come out on top?

BUDDY: That's right, Joh—

JOHNNY: (*cutting* BUDDY *off*) It's been a long season. You've had some key injuries. What's the one thing, Buddy, that you think has made this team so successful?

BUDDY: Well, Johnny—

JOHNNY: (*cutting him off*) Lots of hard work. Lots of team spirit. Lots of hustle and muscle. Is that the way you see it, Buddy?

BUDDY: Actually, I—

JOHNNY: You don't win if you don't play hard. Isn't that right?

BUDDY: (*trying to get a word in*) That's right, Johnny. I think—

JOHNNY: In the words of another great Woodchuck, Michel La Rue, "You win if you c'n. You lose if you choose." Isn't that the way you guys played it all season?

BUDDY: (*fast*) Sure. But we've always tried to—

JOHNNY: Dig, dig, dig. Push, push, push. That's the way you guys played. From the last place in September to the league champion. It's just simply amazing.

BUDDY: (*very fast*) That's right, Johnny. We had hoped to start the—

JOHNNY: Now it's going to be number one for you guys. The start of a hockey legend.

BUDDY: Yes, it makes all of us feel—

JOHNNY: And what about that breakaway you had at the end of the second period? That was some shot with you guys down four. Did you think, Buddy, that that first goal was ever going to be put into the net?

BUDDY: Well, we had our strategy all—

JOHNNY: And then scoring three times in the third period to force the game into overtime! That must be the highlight of your hockey career. You played a fantastic game. How do you feel about it?

BUDDY: In a word, I—

JOHNNY: Listen, Buddy, I don't want to take too much of your valuable time. I know you want to be with your teammates celebrating.

BUDDY: That's true, Joh—

JOHNNY: But just one more word from you before you start dumping all that sticky pop over each other's heads. (*He laughs.*) What can you tell our young listeners out there—the nation's future, Buddy Howler—that might someday help them win their league championship?

BUDDY: (*speaking fast*) To start with, Johnny, I'd like to—

JOHNNY: I know it's a lot to do with winning and hard work. But it's got to be something more than just that. What is it? Tell us.

BUDDY: Well, one aspect certainly is—

JOHNNY: Don't be afraid to say what you really think. Everybody's listening, Buddy. They want to hear what "the Great Howler" has to say.

BUDDY: The most impor—

JOHNNY: And don't let me start putting words into your mouth. Let 'em hear it straight from the heart.

BUDDY: Well, Johnny—

JOHNNY: Go ahead. I know you guys are better shooters on the ice than off. (*He laughs.*) Not like us announcers. But go ahead. Shoot. I'm listening.

BUDDY: Actually, I think—

JOHNNY: The kids out there are listening, too.

BUDDY: (*very fast*) What's really important when playing any sport—

JOHNNY: Well, Buddy, I think we've run out of time. Sorry. It's been fun. I know you always have a lot to say. (*We hear a pop can opening.*) Maybe we can talk some other... Hey! (*We hear pop being poured over* JOHNNY'S *head.*) Hey! (*He laughs half-heartedly.*) That's a good joke, folks. Buddy, in his excitement at helping the Woodchucks win their first divisional title, has just dumped a can of pop all over my head. (*Another can is opened and dumped over his head.* JOHNNY *laughs weakly.*) I thought you guys only dumped pop on your teammates' heads. (*Another can is opened and dumped on* JOHNNY'S *head.*)

BUDDY: That's right, Johnny. (*Yet another can is dumped over* JOHNNY'S *head.*)

JOHNNY: Gee, that stuff sure stings. (*Another can is*

*dumped on his head.*) That's not so funny, Buddy. Hey! What are you guys doing? (*He tries to laugh.*) Three of Johnny's teammates have just lifted me up and… Hey! Hey, where are you taking me? Where are you taking…. (*We hear the sound of a microphone dropping. Pause.*)

BUDDY: (*slowly*) Actually, Johnny, I think the message I'd like to give to our young people listening to tonight's game (*sound starts to fade out*) is that enjoyment of a sport is far more worthwhile than simply having a successful hockey career….

▲▼▶▼▶▲▼▶▼▶▲▼▶▼▶▲▼▶▼▶▶

# TV OR NOT TV?—THAT IS THE QUESTION

## by Bill Majeski

This is the kind of comedy skit we are used to seeing on TV shows like *Saturday Night Live* or *Kids in the Hall*. It's short, silly, and fun to do.

## CHARACTERS

ANNOUNCER (male or female; onstage or offstage)
JERRY, the husband, in his forties
LILLIAN, the wife, approximately the same age

## SETTING

Living room. Chairs, telephone, TV set, or large box with back toward audience, simulating a TV set.

ANNOUNCER: Recently a team of sociologists offered a typical family a cash prize and a week-long vacation in Bermuda if they didn't watch television for a full week. Nice offer, but could the average American family refrain from TV for seven full days? Could you? Let's see what happens when Jerry and Lillian take a shot at winning some money and an all-expense paid vacation by abstaining from watching the tube.

OPENING: *Stage is empty.* JERRY *walks in, gazes at the blank TV set, and nervously sits down in a chair opposite it.* LILLIAN *comes in and sits in a chair across the way.*

LILLIAN: Don't you dare turn on that set, Jerry. I've never been to Bermuda.

JERRY: What's so great about Bermuda? I'd just as soon go to Fargo, North Dakota.

LILLIAN: Fargo, North Dakota? What have they got there?

JERRY: Television, for one thing.

LILLIAN: Now stop talking like that. Only one more day to go and we get that money and the trip.

JERRY: Money, money, money. Everybody thinks of money. What about enjoying life?

LILLIAN: We'll enjoy it more with money on a cruise to Bermuda.

JERRY: (*disgruntled*) Yeah, yeah.

SOUND EFFECT: *Phone rings.* LILLIAN *answers it.*

LILLIAN: (*calling to* JERRY) Don't you go near that TV.

JERRY: Yeah, yeah.

LILLIAN: (*into phone*) Hello? Oh, hi, Mabel. (JERRY *gets up and starts pacing back and forth.* LILLIAN *keeps a watchful eye on him.*) No fooling? What colour? Purple. How much? Well, I must say the price is right.

JERRY: Price is Right! (*starts toward* TV)

LILLIAN: Jerry… (*Gives him hard look; he sits down. Into phone:*) Really? Well, you know that sibling rivalry business. Guess it's just another family feud.

JERRY: Family Feud! (*starts for TV*)

LILLIAN: (*warning him*) Sit down, Jerry. (*He does so, reluctantly. Into phone:*) Well, it's hard to take sides. Guess she's just wrestling with her conscience.

JERRY: Wrestling. Saturday night wrestling! Midgets from the Orient. Sumo wrestlers from Japan! (*He looks at* LILLIAN *and slumps back into his chair.*)

LILLIAN: (*into phone*) Really? Nothing serious I hope. Where? Medical Center?

JERRY: Medical Center? (*grabs stomach*) I'm getting

sick! (*He starts toward TV, but* LILLIAN *has her eye on him.*)

LILLIAN: Sit down. You're not sick. And they've got that set monitored. Don't touch it! I want to see Bermuda! (*He sits back down and she resumes her conversation.*) He always has his sense of humour. Right. He finds a laugh in everything.

JERRY: Laugh-In? (*Looks at* LILLIAN *and sits back in chair.*)

LILLIAN: (*into phone*) No fooling? The bank said that? That puts the whole deal in jeopardy.

JERRY: Jeopardy?! Alex Trebek! What is this happening to me for?

LILLIAN: (*into phone*) She did? Wow! That's a lot of money. She really hit the jackpot.

JERRY: Jackpot! Will you get off that phone?!

LILLIAN: (*Shushes him and continues talking.*) Right. Well, they say if you wait long enough you'll strike it rich.

JERRY: Strike it Rich! (*starts for the TV set*)

LILLIAN: (*shouting at him*) Sit down! Where's your self-control?

JERRY: (*automatically*) Self-control! (*stops and thinks*)

No, that's no show. What am I getting excited about that for? (*He slumps back into chair.*)

LILLIAN: (*into phone*) Yes, I heard that. The boy is a real terror. She calls him a young Frankenstein!

JERRY: Young Frankenstein! Starring Gene Wilder, Peter Boyle, and Marty Feldman. (*Starts toward TV set. She points her finger at him and he sits back down.*)

LILLIAN: (*to* JERRY) I want to see Bermuda! Just a while longer.

JERRY: (*disgruntled*) Yeah, yeah.

LILLIAN: (*into phone*) Hmmm … Well, maybe we can make it then. What night? Monday night? (JERRY *leaps from his seat, snaps on the set, watches it, and then kicks in the TV set.*)

JERRY: Monday Night Football! (*looks at watch*) We made it! Bermuda, here we come!

LILLIAN: No we didn't. You peeked at the set. No Bermuda.

JERRY: No Bermuda?

LILLIAN: (*sympathetically*) No … but you tried your best, Jerry.

JERRY: Yeah, but I blew it.

LILLIAN: (*She embraces him.*) Well, they say Fargo, North Dakota is nice this time of year. (*They embrace at curtain or blackout.*)

▲ ▷ ▶ ▲ ▽ ▶ ▷ ▲ ▷ ▶ ▲ ▽ ▶ ▷ ▲ ▽ ▶ ▷ ▶

# IF I HAD $1 000 000

by Steven Page and Ed Robertson

In Readers' Theatre a piece of writing is read dramatically. It can be a song, a poem, a story—any type of writing. One reader usually takes the part of the narrator, who explains what is happening. Another reader reads the dialogue with lots of feeling and expression.

Try dramatizing these song lyrics written by two members of The Barenaked Ladies, who are neither ladies nor naked.

If I had $1 000 000 (If I had $1 000 000)
I'd buy you a house (I would buy you a house)
If I had $1 000 000 (If I had $1 000 000)
I'd buy you furniture for your house
   (Maybe a nice chesterfield or an ottoman)
If I had $1 000 000 (If I had $1 000 000)
I'd buy you a K-Car (a nice Reliant automobile)
If I had $1 000 000 I'd buy your love.

If I had $1 000 000
I'd build a tree fort in our yard
If I had $1 000 000
You could help, it wouldn't be that hard
If I had $1 000 000
Maybe we could put a refrigerator in there
Wouldn't that be fabulous.

If I had $1 000 000 (If I had $1 000 000)
I'd buy you a fur coat (but not a real fur coat, that's
    cruel)
If I had $1 000 000 (If I had $1 000 000)
I'd buy you an exotic pet (Like a llama or an emu)
If I had $1 000 000 (If I had $1 000 000)
I'd buy you John Merrick's remains (All them crazy
    elephant bones)
If I had $1 000 000 I'd buy your love.

If I had $1 000 000
We wouldn't have to walk to the store
If I had $1 000 000
We'd take a limousine 'cause it costs more
If I had $1 000 000
We wouldn't have to eat Kraft Dinner.
But we would. We'd actually make the tree fort
    from the first chorus out of it. Mmm.

If I had $1 000 000 (If I had $1 000 000)
I'd buy you a green dress (but not a real green
  dress, that's cruel)
If I had $1 000 000 (If I had $1 000 000)
I'd buy you some art (a Picasso or a Garfunkel)
If I had $1 000 000 (If I had $1 000 000)
I'd buy you a monkey (haven't you always wanted
  a monkey?)
If I had $1 000 000 I'd buy your love.

If I had $1 000 000, If I had $1 000 000
If I had $1 000 000, If I had $1 000 000
I'd be rich.

# 4

# Short Plays

▲▼▶▼▲▼▶▼▲▼▶▼▲▼▶▼▲▼▶▼▲▶▶

Interacting with other actors, you discover that the group is greater than its individual parts. It's like being on a sports team, but without the competition. Even if you are sitting while reading aloud your part, you will be responding to the voices and emotions of your fellow actors. Of course, it's more lifelike if you can stand up and move around as you perform a piece.

▲▼▶▼▲▼▶▼▲▼▶▼▲▼▶▼▲▼▶▼▲▶▶

▲ ▼ ▼ ▶ ▲ ▼ ▶ ▼ ▶ ▲ ▼ ▶ ▼ ▶ ▲ ▼ ▶ ▼ ▶ ▶

# THE HODJA SPEAKS

## by Barbara Winther

In Turkish folklore, Hodja is a character of wit and mischief. Here, he challenges his wife to a contest to see who can stay silent the longest.

## CHARACTERS

NARRATOR (offstage voice)
THE HODJA
WIFE
THIEF
MUSTAFA

BEFORE RISE: *Music. Lights are dimmed.*

NARRATOR: (*from offstage, on microphone*) For hundreds of years in the country of Turkey, tales have been told about Nasr-ed-Din Hodja, a legendary character. Although he was not always as wise as he thought, neither was he the fool that many considered him. But whether wise or foolish, he always had something to say that was amusing and thought-provoking, as in this tale about feeding the donkey. (*Turkish music is heard as curtain opens, and lights come up.*)

SETTING: *Inside the Hodja's house in a Turkish village. Low table with brass vase on it is centre; two large pillows are on floor nearby. Up right is a trunk with valuables inside. Right exit is to kitchen; left exit to street.*

AT RISE: *Stage is empty. Music fades as* HODJA, *wearing a large turban, and* WIFE *enter right.*

THE HODJA: Every day I go outside (*pointing left*) to feed the donkey. It is time you did it.

WIFE: (*shocked*) That is a man's job.

HODJA: Where is it written a wife should not feed a donkey?

WIFE: How should I know? You are the learned Hodja.

HODJA: Then I say that somewhere it must be written, "Men or women may feed donkeys."

WIFE: (*indignantly*) But I have other things to do. Besides, when have you cooked the meals (*indicating right*) or cleaned the house?

HODJA: (*calmly*) I cannot remember.

WIFE: Because never have you done so.

HODJA: Well, neither has the donkey.

WIFE: Of course not!

HODJA: Then, since neither I nor the donkey does housework, yet you feed me, why should you not also feed the donkey?

WIFE: (*exasperated*) But, I—you—(*throws up arms*) I will not be tricked by you.

HODJA: Excellent! I would not want a wife who could be tricked, even by her husband. (*He pauses as he pulls on beard, deep in thought, then smiles and claps hands.*) I have the solution.

WIFE: (*warily*) Tell me what it is.

HODJA: We will have a contest—a silence contest. Whoever speaks first will have to feed the donkey.

WIFE: (*considering*) You are rarely silent. I do not believe you could keep quiet, unless you decide to take a nap.

HODJA: (*smiling slyly*) When value is to be gained, I have much determination.

WIFE: We shall see.

HODJA: The contest will start at the count of three.

WIFE: All right.

HODJA: One, two, three. (*They sit on pillows. After a moment,* HODJA *points in amazement at someone in the audience.* WIFE *follows his stare, shrugs, and just as she opens her mouth to question him, she claps hand over mouth. Next,* HODJA *points to imaginary bug crawling on floor.* WIFE *examines closely, but sees nothing. She starts to speak, then claps hand over mouth.* HODJA *leaps up, looks at ceiling in terror.* WIFE *follows his gaze. He holds hands over head and cringes.* WIFE *starts to speak, claps hand over mouth, shakes her finger angrily at him, and exits left.* HODJA *yawns and rubs eyes. He carries pillow upstage, stretches, lies down and falls asleep.* THIEF, *carrying sack over shoulder, enters left, stealthily, not seeing* HODJA.)

THIEF: Nobody is home. This is a good time for me to steal whatever is in that trunk. (*Tiptoes over to trunk, opens it, and begins to load contents into sack, looking warily at doors from time to time. He notices vase on table.*) That is a fine vase. I shall take it also. (*Picks up vase, accidentally drops it. At the sound,* HODJA *awakens, jumps up in alarm, but does not speak.* THIEF *drops sack and sinks to knees, bowing head to floor.*) Oh-h-h, it is the Hodja, the wise and powerful one. I did not know you lived here. Please forgive me. I will replace everything I have stolen. Forgive me, and I will leave your house with a changed heart, never to steal again. (HODJA *opens mouth to speak, claps hand over it, shakes head, and returns to sit on pillow.* THIEF, *surprised, rises.*) Do you not forgive me? (*Pause.* THIEF *looks at audience and shrugs. Aside:*) The Hodja appears to have lost his voice. (*Crosses to* HODJA *and waves hand before his eyes.*) You say nothing, and you do nothing. Perhaps you have suddenly turned into a statue. Hm-m-m. Since you have no objection to your treasures being stolen, I shall also steal your handsome kavuk, symbol of wisdom. (*Removes* HODJA'S *turban and places it on his own head. Then, throwing sack over shoulder, he quickly exits left.* HODJA, *feeling his head, jumps up angrily.* MUSTAFA *enters, carrying dish.*)

MUSTAFA: Good day to you, Nasr-ed-Din Hodja. My father sends this plate of delicious pilaf for you to eat. (HODJA *rushes to him, gesturing wildly and pointing left.*) Is something wrong, Hodja? (HODJA *runs to trunk and points inside.* MUSTAFA *looks.*) Yes, that is a trunk. (HODJA *jumps inside trunk and waves his arms about.*) What are you doing in the trunk? (HODJA *leaps out and runs to table, pointing to it.* MUSTAFA *looks confused.*) Yes, that is a table. (HODJA *jumps on table.*) What are you doing on the table? (HODJA *runs to doorway and points to it.*) Yes, that is a doorway. I, Mustafa, came through your doorway. (HODJA *runs back to trunk and points furiously.*) No, I do not wish to get into your trunk. (HODJA *points to table.*) No, I do not want to stand on your table. I came to make you a present of this pilaf. (HODJA *shakes fists in frustration.*) Hodja, do not be angry with me. Have you lost your voice? (HODJA *sadly shakes head.*) Has it been stolen? (HODJA *nods emphatically, with great relief.*) Stolen, you say? (*Aside to audience, as* HODJA *points to top of his head:*) Is this what comes from being a learned man? (*to* HODJA) I must go home now. Please tell me where you want me to put the pilaf. (HODJA *continues to point at his head.*) You want it on your head? (HODJA *nods.*) Oh, well (*shrugs*), if that is what you wish. (*Pours pilaf on* HODJA'S *head and runs out left, calling:*) Father, the Hodja thinks his mouth is on top of his head. (MUSTAFA *exits.* WIFE *enters, horrified at the sight of* HODJA *and ransacked trunk.*)

WIFE: Husband, what has happened? (HODJA *shouts with delight.*)

HODJA: I won! I won the contest! You spoke—you will have to feed the donkey.

WIFE: But our treasures have been stolen, your

kavuk is gone, and there is pilaf all over your head.

HODJA: If you had fed my donkey in the first place, this would not have happened.

WIFE: That is true.

HODJA: But now that I have won the contest, not only have you *one* silly, old donkey to feed (*pointing off left*), you have *two*. (*Meekly points to self.* WIFE *bursts into laughter. Curtain closes as Turkish music plays.*)

# FINN McCOOL

## by May Lynch

In this dramatization of an Irish tale, a giant named Cuhullin comes looking for Finn McCool. Finn and his wife, Una, have to think of a way to outwit Cuhullin.

## CHARACTERS

FINN McCOOL
UNA, his wife
OWEN
JOHN
JAMIE } their children
MEG
CELIA
GRANNIE
MRS. O'MALLEY
MRS. SHANE
CUHULLIN

**SETTING:** *The interior of Finn McCool's cabin, on top of Knockmany Mountain, in Ireland.*

**AT RISE:** UNA *stands at a washtub, wringing out a piece of clothing. She places it on top of a basket of laundry at her feet.* OWEN, JAMIE, *and* JOHN *are sitting nearby.*

UNA: There! That's the last of my washing, and I must say it was a big one.

OWEN: I'll say it was. I carried six buckets of water up Knockmany Mountain this morning.

JOHN: And so did Jamie and I. We do it all the time.

OWEN: You didn't carry six buckets, John.

JAMIE: (*laughing*) No, Owen, but you spilled half of yours.

OWEN: I did not, Jamie McCool!

JAMIE: You did, too.

OWEN: (*loudly*) I did not!

UNA: Children! Stop that brawling and squalling. My, I'll be glad when your father, Finn McCool, finds us a spring up here near the house.

JOHN: He says that there's water right out there under those two rocks.

JAMIE: Yes, and he's going to move them someday.

OWEN: (*interrupting*) Someday! Someday! He keeps saying *someday*, but *someday* never comes.

UNA: Owen McCool, don't speak that way of your father. After all, the dear man is very busy and tired—and—and busy. (MEG *and* CELIA *enter.*)

CELIA: Mother! Mother! Guess what!

MEG: Grannie Owen and Mrs. O'Malley and Mrs. Shane are coming up Knockmany Mountain right now.

UNA: Your grannie hasn't been here in a long time. Put on the teakettle, Meg. Celia, dear, lay the cloth. And Owen, hang these things out on the line, like a good boy.

OWEN: I have to do *everything*.

JAMIE: I'll help you. Come on. (*He picks up basket of laundry. The two* BOYS *exit.*)

JOHN: I'll fix the fire. (UNA *and the* GIRLS *tidy up the room, as* JOHN *kneels at fireplace.*)

CELIA: (*at window*) Here they are. I see them coming up the path.

JOHN: (*opening the door*) Welcome, Grannie. Good day, Mrs. Shane. Good health to you, Mrs. O'Malley.

GRANNIE, MRS. O'MALLEY, *and* MRS. SHANE *enter. All exchange greetings. The* GIRLS *kiss* GRANNIE.

GRANNIE: Well, I must say, Knockmany Mountain gets steeper every year. I'm puffing from that long walk.

MRS. O'MALLEY: I am, too. And that wind gets stronger and stronger.

MRS. SHANE: Una, however do you manage in winter when that cold wind howls and blows and screams? Aren't you afraid to be up here?

UNA: (*laughing*) No, indeed. Finn McCool wouldn't live anywhere else in the world. (LADIES *glance at each other with knowing looks.*)

GRANNIE: Where is Finn today?

JOHN: He's somewhere about. He's busy, I guess.

UNA: He's such a busy man, you know.

MRS. SHANE: It's too bad he's too busy to find a spring up here. Those poor lads of yours shouldn't have to carry water all the way up the mountain.

JOHN: We really like to do that, Mrs. Shane. Besides, our father says that someday he is going to let my brothers and me help him split open those rocks out there. There's water under them. (LADIES *shake their heads.*)

**MEG:** Grannie, Mother, Mrs. O'Malley, Mrs. Shane, do sit down and have a cup of tea. (LADIES *sit, as* GIRLS *serve them tea and pass a plate of cakes.*)

**GRANNIE:** It's good to see you, Una. Since Finn built this house on top of the world, we seldom get together.

**MRS. SHANE:** Is it true, Una, that Finn came up here to get away from Cuhullin?

**UNA:** Goodness, no.

**JOHN:** Who is Cuhullin?

**MRS. O'MALLEY:** (*quickly*) Nobody important, John.

**MRS. SHANE:** *Nobody important?* He's a giant. That's who he is.

**JOHN:** Finn McCool, our father, is a giant, too.

**MRS. SHANE:** Oh, but Cuhullin is very strong. There's not a man so strong within a hundred miles of our town of Dungannon.

**GRANNIE:** Except maybe my son-in-law, Finn McCool.

**MRS. SHANE:** The talk around Dungannon right now is that Cuhullin once stamped his foot and all of Ireland shook and trembled.

**JOHN:** Why would he do that?

MRS. SHANE: To show that he had beaten every single giant in Ireland except Finn McCool, whom he can't find.

MRS. O'MALLEY: (*nervously*) I don't like to frighten you, Una, but there is talk in town that Cuhullin is on his way here to find Finn.

GRANNIE: But there's nothing to be afraid of, Una. You can all come down to my cottage and hide until Cuhullin goes away.

MRS. SHANE: Yes, you'd better.

MRS. O'MALLEY: Get the children and Finn right away, Una. My Mr. O'Malley heard only this morning that Cuhullin was thundering toward Dungannon.

MRS. SHANE: They say he'll stamp Finn into pancakes when he finds him.

JOHN: But why?

GRANNIE: It's an old story, John. Finn used to brag about how much stronger he was than Cuhullin. Of course, Cuhullin heard about it and he began to look for Finn McCool.

MRS. O'MALLEY: And he's never found him. Come, Una. Come with us.

UNA: Why, we have nothing to be afraid of. Finn

will take care of us.

LADIES: (*ad lib; excitedly*) Please come right away. We're frightened. (*etc.*)

UNA: No, we'll be perfectly safe. (*Thinks for a moment.*) But I just remembered I must do some baking.

JOHN: You just did your week's baking, Mother. (UNA *starts to mix flour and salt in a bowl, as* GRANNIE *and other* LADIES *rise.*)

UNA: Did I indeed, John? (*to* LADIES) Must you go so soon, ladies? (*They nod and start toward door.*) Finn will be sorry he wasn't here to see you. Come again soon.

GRANNIE: We will, Una. (*aside:*) Poor Finn will be no more. Poor Finn McCool. (*They exit.*)

CELIA: Mother, is it true what they said about Cuhullin? (UNA *shrugs and continues mixing.*)

UNA: (*to herself*) I need some iron skillets. (*Picks up two skillets.*) Here they are.

MEG: I'm scared, Mother.

UNA: (*to herself*) One bite of bread with a skillet in it will take care of Cuhullin. (*She starts to cover the skillets with dough.* FINN *enters.*)

FINN: I'm a dead man. I've been to Dungannon, and

the giant Cuhullin is on his way to town looking for me. He told somebody he'd squeeze me into a sausage.

GIRLS: Is he big?

FINN: Big he is. Too big for me to handle. And *I'm* too big to hide from him.

UNA: You leave everything to me, Finn. I'll handle Cuhullin. Meg, give your father that old long nightdress of mine and find the baby's bonnet in the drawer. (*to* FINN) And *you* put on the night-dress and the bonnet and hide in that bed over there. (*She puts bread into oven.* MEG *exits.*)

FINN: Right here. Hide here in the open? (UNA *nods her head. He exits and returns wearing a long white nightgown and a bonnet. He climbs into bed, as* MEG *re-enters.*)

UNA: Girls, get Jamie and Owen and gather lots of kindling. Then build a great big fire right on the very tip of Knockmany Mountain.

CELIA: But a fire on the mountain means that we are welcoming a stranger. The only stranger is—is Cuhullin.

MEG: I'm too scared to move.

UNA: Go! Get your brothers to help you. (*to* JOHN) You, son, stand where the wind will carry your whistle. As soon as you see Cuhullin coming up the mountain, you must let out your long, loud whistle.

FINN: Ooooh! Ooooh! I'm scared out of my wits. Cuhullin will make a grease spot of me. He'll chew my darling children up alive and carry off my good wife.

UNA: Nonsense! You just listen to my plan. I've already made bread Cuhullin will never forget, and now if I take a cobblestone and make it look like a cheese—(*She sits on edge of bed and whispers in* FINN'S *ear. Both of them burst into loud laughter. She whispers again, pointing to the oven. Loud whistle is heard.*) Cuhullin is coming! (*She pulls the covers around* FINN.) Now keep the bonnet on and remember *who* you are! (*She hands him a stone and a round cheese from the table.*) Now, don't roll on this cheese. (*A loud banging at the door is heard.*)

CUHULLIN: (*shouting from offstage*) Is this where you live, Finn McCool? Open up, if you're a man. (UNA *opens the door, looks surprised.*)

UNA: Well, I wondered if I heard someone at the door. It's so windy I don't always hear people knocking. Come in, stranger. Welcome.

CUHULLIN: (*entering*) Does Finn McCool live here?

UNA: (*sweetly*) He does, indeed.

CUHULLIN: Is he home?

UNA: Dear me, no! He left here an hour ago. Somebody said a giant named Cuhullin was down in Dungannon looking for him. Finn went right down to make pudding out of him.

CUHULLIN: Mm-m-m.

UNA: Did you ever hear of Cuhullin, poor thing?

CUHULLIN: That's me.

UNA: Oh, you poor man. Finn is in a terrible temper. Don't let him find you.

CUHULLIN: I've been wanting to meet him for years. I notice he doesn't let *me* find *him*.

UNA: Well, wait for him then. But don't say I didn't warn you.

CUHULLIN: I'll wait.

UNA: Don't be nervous. Here, to keep yourself from being scared, and while you're waiting, would you do me a favour? (*He nods.*) Would you turn the house around? Finn always turns it around in the fall when the wind blows at the door. It makes it warmer in winter.

CUHULLIN: Turn the house? Nothing easier. (*He exits. A loud noise is heard from offstage.* UNA *goes to the door.* FINN *groans.*)

UNA: (*calling*) That's better. Thank you very much. Now, would you do something else? Finn has been meaning to pull those rocks apart and find us a spring, but he hurried off, and I do need water. (*She steps back toward* FINN *as a loud crash is heard.*) Good heavens! He pulled apart those rocks with his bare hands and made a spring! (FINN *groans.* CUHULLIN *enters.*)

CUHULLIN: What now?

UNA: That's a good little job finished. Now you come and have a bite to eat. Even though you think Finn is your enemy, he would want me to be kind to anyone in our home. Here's a cup of tea and I have some hot bread right in the oven. (*She takes out loaves of bread.* CUHULLIN *bites into the bread.*)

CUHULLIN: Blood and thunder! I just broke my two front teeth. What did you give me to eat, woman?

UNA: Only what Finn always eats. He and our little child in the bed have these biscuits all the time. (*She indicates the bed.*) Try another one.

CUHULLIN: Jumping shamrocks. My teeth are ruined. Take this stuff away. What a toothache! (*holds jaw*)

FINN: (*in a deep voice*) Give me something to eat. I'm

hungry! (UNA *takes a loaf of bread to* FINN, *and he pretends to eat it.*) Yum!

CUHULLIN: (*amazed*) I'd like to see that child. He must be some boy!

UNA: Get up, dearie, and show the man that you're Finn's little son.

FINN: (*jumping out of bed*) Are you strong like my father?

CUHULLIN: Toads and snakes! What a gigantic child!

FINN: Are you strong? Can you squeeze water from a stone? My father can, and so can I. (*He hands white stone to* CUHULLIN, *who squeezes it.*) Ah, you *can't* do it. (FINN *takes stone, throws it on bed, then picks up cheese, unseen by* CUHULLIN, *and squeezes it until water drips from it.*) My father, Finn McCool, taught me to do that. He can stamp a man to pancakes.

UNA: Into bed, son. You'll never grow strong and big like your father if you don't get your rest.

CUHULLIN: (*nervously*) I think I'd better go. I never saw the like of that child. What must his father be like!

FINN: Will Father hurt that little man, Mother?

UNA: No, dearie. (*to* CUHULLIN) You are the lucky

one that Finn isn't home. That temper of his! (CUHULLIN *exits, running.* FINN *and* UNA *laugh. The* CHILDREN *come running in.*)

MEG: Mother, what did you do to Cuhullin?

JOHN: He was holding his jaw and crying about a toothache.

OWEN: I heard him muttering about pancakes and a baby giant.

JAMIE: I watched from the bushes. He pulled those rocks apart one—two—three. And now we have a spring.

UNA: And he turned the house around. It's warmer already.

MEG: How did you do it, Mother?

FINN: Ah, your mother is a clever woman. She makes rocks out of cheese.

UNA: Your father fooled him. Cuhullin tried to squeeze water from a rock, but Finn squeezed water from *cheese*. Cuhullin never knew the difference.

FINN: And she put iron skillets into her bread and served them for biscuits.

UNA: But your father fooled him. He just nibbled around the crust.

OWEN: Why are you wearing that silly outfit, Father?

UNA: You should have seen how your father fooled him, pretending he was a baby giant. (*All laugh.*)

FINN: Now if somebody will help me out of this nightgown, I'll lie down and have a rest. A busy man like me gets very tired. (*Curtain.*)

▲ ▼ ▶ ▼ ▶ ▲ ▼ ▶ ▼ ▶ ▲ ▼ ▶ ▼ ▶ ▲ ▼ ▶ ▼ ▶ ▶

# HARRIET TUBMAN—
# THE SECOND MOSES

## by Aileen Fisher

Harriet Tubman escaped from slavery in Maryland and earned her nickname as she helped to smuggle hundreds of other slaves to freedom on the Underground Railroad. This play is punctuated by traditional black spirituals sung by a chorus. If you have no chorus, you can use taped music.

## CHARACTERS

HARRIET TUBMAN
THREE GIRLS
THREE BOYS
CHORUS (any number)

1ST GIRL:  When Harriet Tubman
Was six years old
Her childhood was over.

Up till then
She had a carefree life
on the plantation.

HARRIET: The older children were
already working in the fields.
My mother was cook at the Big House.
My father picked cotton or
worked in the piney woods.

2ND GIRL: "Some day," her mother said,
"we will be free.
The master promised me."

HARRIET: I thought very little
about being free.
I thought this was the way
things had to be:
Some people lived in fine houses,
had carriages with horses;
the rest of us lived in cabins
and worked on the plantation,
always in fear of the overseer
who would snap a whip with leather
thongs.

1ST BOY: When Harriet turned six,
the master decided she was
strong enough to work for money.
He hired her out to a lady
to take care of her baby

and clean the house.

**HARRIET:** She was not a kind lady.
She used to whip my legs
when I was slow or
when I looked out of the window.

**3RD GIRL:** One day Harriet was so tired
she fell asleep rocking the baby.
The lady sent her back to the Big House.
Harriet cried with joy
to be back home again.

CHORUS *sings "Swing Low, Sweet Chariot."*

**2ND BOY:** The master said,
"You're strong for your age.
You'll be a good field hand."

**HARRIET:** Field work was not easy—
Picking cotton, cotton, cotton all day,
with the sun burning down
sometimes making me dizzy.
But I was glad to be with my people
again.
When the overseer could not hear us,
we would talk and sing.

CHORUS *sings "My Lord, What a Morning."*

**3RD BOY:** Often the talk was about freedom,
a word that sounded like music
to Harriet.

**HARRIET:** By the time I was twelve,
I was handling a plough.
Sometimes when the master
was in need of money,
he rented my father and me out
to work for a neighbour.

**1ST BOY:** They cut trees,
trimmed off the branches,
and skidded the logs to the loading place.

**HARRIET:** When I was fifteen,
a black man who was free
came to work on the plantation
for pay.
His name was John Tubman.
We liked to work together.
After a time, John and I
got married. But in a few
months, we were not getting along well.
We didn't agree
on the one great thought
that burned in my heart:
FREEDOM!

CHORUS *sings "Go Down, Moses."*

**1ST GIRL:** John had his papers—
He was already free.
He didn't worry about Harriet
longing for freedom.

HARRIET: Suddenly, life changed again for me.
The master died and
all the slaves on the plantation
worried about what would happen:
Would we get a cruel, new master?
Would we be sold?
Would our families be separated?
The master had promised my mother
her freedom, but he died
before he signed the papers.
What would happen to us?

1ST BOY: They often heard of a
slave escaping from
one of the plantations.
Sometimes a slave would make
his way north to safety.
Sometimes slave-catchers
and their dogs
picked up the trail,
caught him, and
brought him back
to be flogged.

HARRIET: Oh, I knew the dangers,
yet the thought of freedom
was always with me,
glowing like the North Star.
One night, without telling anyone,
I took my brother's shoes

and my father's coat,
put some victuals[1] in a sack,
and headed for the swamp.

CHORUS *sings "O, Shenandoah!"*

2ND BOY: Part of Maryland
near Chesapeake Bay
where the plantation lay
was swampy lowland,
with heavy timber and
thick tangles of brush
and rotting logs.

3RD GIRL: Harriet had to push through
this wet, unfriendly country,
away from roads where slave-catchers
might be lurking.
She had to travel by night
with no map to follow,
only the North Star to guide her
to the Promised Land.

HARRIET: If I could get to Philadelphia,
I knew I would be safe.
I was headed for a farm that
welcomed runaway slaves.

CHORUS *sings "My Lord, What a Morning."*

3RD BOY: Early on the second morning,
she reached the farm.

She was weary and splattered with mud.
They took her in, fed her, and
gave her dry clothes.
They showed her a place to hide
in the barn under the hay.

**HARRIET:** They told me where the next
house was on the way
to Philadelphia. "Now you're
on the Underground Railroad,"
they said.

**2ND GIRL:** The Underground Railroad
was a secret system to
help slaves reach the
free states and Canada.

**1ST BOY:** One farmer
gave her a ride in his wagon
under a load of corn.
Another farmer, a free black man,
gave her men's clothes to wear.

**3RD GIRL:** Finally, after many gruelling days,
she reached Philadelphia,
where she found refuge
in the home of a Quaker
who ran a "station" on the Underground.
He sent her on to the home
of another Quaker
where she would be safe.

CHORUS *sings "Nobody Knows the Trouble I've Seen."*

HARRIET: My new mistress
was kind in every way.
She taught me
the things I should know
about doing housework,
and she paid me in cash.

I saved my money so I could go back
south
to rescue my family and friends.
Oh, I knew it was dangerous.
There was a reward posted
for my capture,
a reward of thousands of dollars
for me, dead or alive!

But I knew I had been chosen
to be a second Moses,
to lead my people to freedom.

CHORUS *sings "Go Down, Moses."*

HARRIET: "Go down, Moses," I sang my own
words.
"Go down, Moses,
Way down in Maryland.
Tell the old masters
to let my people go!"

**3RD BOY:** In all, Harriet went back south
nineteen times.
She led more than three hundred
of her people
from slavery to freedom,
without ever being caught
or losing a "passenger"
on the Underground Railroad.

**HARRIET:** The hardest trip
was the one I made
to fetch my old mother and father.
They were weary and the way
was long.
Slave-catchers watched for "Moses"
at every crossroad.
We had many narrow escapes.
But we finally reached
our promised land—
the little house I had
bought in New York state.
There we found the freedom
I had dreamed of
for so long....

CHORUS *sings "Swing Low, Sweet Chariot," or any
other spiritual.*

1. **victuals:** supplies of food

# ACKNOWLEDGEMENTS

Permission to reprint copyright material is gratefully acknowledged. Every reasonable effort to trace the copyright holders of materials appearing in this book has been made. Information that will enable the publisher to rectify any error or omission will be welcomed.

CAUTION: Professionals and amateurs are hereby warned that all the plays in this anthology are fully protected by copyright and are subject to royalty. All dramatic rights, including professional, amateur, motion picture, recitation, lecturing, public reading, radio and television broadcasting, as well as rights of translation into foreign languages, are strictly reserved by the copyright holders listed below. Applications for performance rights or other use of plays must be directed to the individual copyright holder at the address indicated in that play's acknowledgement.

**Mirrors** by David W. Booth and Charles J. Lundy from *Improvisation: Learning Through Drama* by David Booth and Charles Lundy. Reprinted by permission of Harcourt Brace & Company Canada, 55 Horner Ave., Toronto, Ontario M8Z 4X6. **It Could Be Worse**, © by Larry Swartz from his book *Dramathemes*. Reprinted with permission of Pembroke Publishers, 538 Hood Road, Markham, Ontario L3R 3K9. **Fortunately/Unfortunately** by Peter Moore from *When are we going to have MORE DRAMA?* Copyright © 1988 by Peter Moore. Published by Thomas Nelson Australia, 102 Dodds Street, South Melbourne, Victoria 3205, Australia. **Tongue Twisters** collected by Anna Scher and Charles Verrall from *200 + Ideas for Drama* © 1992 by Anna Scher and Charles Verrall. Portions previously © 1975 under the title *100 + Ideas for Drama* and © 1977 under the title *Another 100 + Ideas for Drama*. David Higham Associates, London. **I Had to Go** from *Runaways* by Elizabeth Swados. Copyright © 1979 by Swados Enterprises, Inc. Used by permission of Bantam Books, a division of Bantam Doubleday Dell Publishing Group, Inc., 1540 Broadway, New York, NY 10036 USA. **Little League Dreamer** by Peg Kehret from *Winning Monologs for Young Actors* by Peg Kehret © 1986 Meriwether Publishing Ltd., 885 Elkton Drive, Colorado

Springs, CO 80907. **Waitress!** by Vernon Howard reprinted by permission of Sterling Publishing Co., Inc., 387 Park Ave. S., New York, NY 10016. From *Humorous Monologues* by Vernon Howard © 1973, 1955 by Sterling Publishing Co., Inc. **The Life and Times of Humpty Dumpty** by Martha Bolton adapted by permission of Sterling Publishing Co., Inc., 387 Park Ave. S., NY, NY 10016. From *Humorous Monologues* by Martha Bolton, © 1989 by Martha Bolton. **Calvin and Hobbes** by Bill Watterson © 1993 Watterson. Reprinted with permission of Universal Press Syndicate. All rights reserved. **Envy** by Joan Sturkie and Marsh Cassady adapted from "Teens Who Envy" from *Acting It Out* by Joan Sturkie and Marsh Cassady. Copyright © 1990 by Resource Publications, Inc., 160 E. Virginia St., #290, San Jose, CA 95112, USA. **Who's on First?** by Bud Abbott and Lou Costello was presented in 1956 to the Baseball Hall of Fame and Museum, Cooperstown, New York. **Jock Talk: A Radio Interview** by Jeff Siamon reprinted by permission of the author. For performance rights, contact Jeff Siamon, 8 Chapel Street, Box 730, Brighton, Ontario, K0K 1H0. **TV or Not TV?—That is the Question** by Bill Majeski from *Doubletalk: 50 Comedy Duets for Actors* by Bill Majeski © 1990 Meriwether Publishing Ltd., 885 Elkton Drive, Colorado Springs, CO 80907. **If I Had $1 000 000** by Steven Page and Ed Robertson [from the CD *Gordon* by The Barenaked Ladies] © 1988 WB Music Corp. & Treat Baker Music. All rights administered by WB Music Corp. All rights reserved. Used by permission. **The Hodja Speaks** by Barbara Winther, is reprinted by permission from *The Big Book of Folktale Plays*, edited by Sylvia E. Kamerman. Copyright © 1991 by Plays, Inc., Publishers, 120 Boylston St., Boston, MA 02116 USA. **Finn McCool** by May Lynch, is reprinted by permission from *Dramatized Folktales of the World*, edited by Sylvia E. Kamerman. Copyright © 1971 by Plays, Inc., Publishers, 120 Boylston St., Boston, MA 02116 USA. **Harriet Tubman—The Second Moses** by Aileen Fisher, is reprinted by permission from *Plays of Black Americans*, edited by Sylvia E. Kamerman. Copyright © 1987, 1991 by Plays, Inc., Publishers, 120 Boylston St., Boston, MA 02116 USA.

# THE EDITORS

**Sharon Siamon** is the author of ten novels for young readers as well as reviews and plays. She has been involved in numerous educational publications and is a contributing editor for *Owl* magazine. A former teacher, now living in Brighton, Ontario, she enjoys working with students and teachers in writing workshops.

**James Barry** is Chairman of the English Department at Brebeuf College School, North York, Ontario. He is the editor of the poetry anthologies *Themes on the Journey*, *Departures*, *Side by Side*, and *Poetry Express*, as well as an annual student writing anthology, *Triple Bronze*. Besides teaching, his special interests are sports (especially hockey), music, and student writing.